Pushing On

*Daughter Donates Half of Liver
to Mother Out of Love*

Pushing On

*Daughter Donates Half of Liver
to Mother Out of Love*

Pearl Lambert
Vicki Lambert

PUBLISHED BY

Mother Daughter Love Publications
Alexandria, VA

Published by
Mother Daughter Love Publications
Alexandria, VA
ISBN: 978-0-9984078-1-4

Copyright © 2017

Vicki Lambert
Mother Daughter Love Publications
PO Box 90342
Alexandria, VA 22309
www.pushingon.us
MotherDaughterLovePublications@gmail.com
703-625-5218

All rights reserved. No part of this book may be reproduced, stored in a retrieval system, or transmitted in any form or by any means, electronic, mechanical, photocopying, recording, scanning, or otherwise, without the prior written permission of the publisher.

DISCLAIMER

All the material contained in this book is provided for educational and informational purposes only. No responsibility can be taken for any results or outcomes resulting from the use of this material.

While every attempt has been made to provide information that is both accurate and effective, the author does not assume any responsibility for the accuracy or use/misuse of this information.

*"I always thought I would help you grow up
into being the woman that I wanted you to be.
However, being your mother taught me so many
things and made me the woman that I am today."*

— ANONYMOUS

Acknowledgements

To God Be the Glory for the Gift of Life

Our sincere and unending appreciation to friends, family members, doctors, and nurses who supported us before and after the transplants.

Our BIG appreciation to the entire medical team at Georgetown University Hospital, the entire medical team at DaVita Dialysis Center, Duke Street, in Alexandria, VA, the Washington Transplant Community, the National Kidney Foundation Family, my two children, all Pearl's brothers and sisters, nieces and nephews, first, second, third, and fourth cousins, close friends Doris P., I. Dixon, C. Terry, Diane P., and the Walnut Grove Baptist Church.

Our profound appreciation to the donor family who reached out to us through the Washington Transplant Community, http://www.beadonor.org/

We are extremely grateful that a kidney was donated to Pearl. Thanks to those who donate one thing or the other to humanity.

Contents

Foreword 11

Chapter 1: Shock! Where It All Started 17

Chapter 2: Fear Again? 25

Chapter 3: Vicki's Sacrificial Love 35

Chapter 4: A Second Successful Transplant 45

Chapter 5: A Family Like No Other 57

Chapter 6: Our Volunteer Activities 65

Chapter 7: Now Is Your Turn: Donate! 69

Chapter 8: Various Media Reports About Our Story .. 75

Epilogue 91

About the Authors 97

Foreword

A daughter is the happy memories of the past, the joyful moments of the present, and the hope and promise of the future—Author Unknown

My name is Pearl Lambert. My daughter and I are driven to share our story to help educate people about organ donation, liver disease, kidney disease, health, wellness and the GREATNESS OF GOD.

I was a very busy person. I worked two jobs, one as a custodian of Fairfax County Public Schools (FCPS) for 25 years. I also had a part time job as a bus assistant working for children under the age of four in Fauquier County. I would get up at 6:30 a.m. and work from 7a.m. – 1 p.m. then head 40 miles to my full-time job in FCPS and work from 3 p.m. – 11 p.m. at night.

I had always maintained a part-time job most of my life to make ends meet. I worked hard to raise my two children: Ronald Lambert, Jr., who is a survivor of cerebral palsy, and Vicki Lambert.

I've attended Walnut Grove Baptist Church for many years. I was a choir member for the Voices of Praise for over 25 years. I was always on the go. I would attend church activities, attend family functions, and help others who needed me. Walnut Grove Baptist Church is my family church. My mother and grandfather helped to build it and donated the land to the church over 100 years ago. The church didn't have a building, and the members would meet on a bench that was placed under big, beautiful trees that my grandfather had on his land. As the church grew, my grandfather donated the land so a building could be built for my family and local community members to attend church. I can remember that we didn't have heating and central air. My grandfather would warm up the church with an old-fashioned wood stove. More than 100 years later, our family church has grown and expanded. I remain close to this church because it gives me so many memories of my mother and family and how we stayed close to help each other and families in our local community. Many members at my church were very supportive while I was sick. They prayed many days and many nights that God would give me the strength to get well through all my operations.

At 51, I had reached the ultimate prime of my life. Then I discovered I had a rare liver disease and would need a liver transplant—as soon as possible because my liver could fail and I could not be in this world anymore.

On December 18, 2002, my daughter Vicki donated half of her liver to me. She unselfishly volunteered to give me a portion of her liver so I could survive. In the United States, there is a shortage of organ donors among minorities. According to a study at www.organdonor.gov, African Americans are three times more likely than Caucasians to suffer from end-stage renal (kidney) disease, often as the result of high blood pressure and other conditions that can damage the kidneys—almost 34 percent more than the 101,000 people on the national waiting list. Among African Americans there are many people waiting to receive a liver transplant. It's also reported that today many people have kidney failure and are either on dialysis or waiting to receive a kidney transplant. The study also said that although organs are not matched according to race/ethnicity, and people of different races frequently match one another, all individuals waiting for an organ transplant will have a better chance of receiving one if there are large numbers of donors from their racial/ethnic background. This is because compatible blood types and tissue markers—critical qualities for donor/recipient matching—are more likely to be found among members of the same ethnicity. A greater diversity of donors may potentially increase access to transplantation for everyone.

After surviving my liver transplant in 2002, I was shocked to find out that I was beginning to have kidney failure. My medical team informed me that I would need dialysis to survive, and that a kidney needed to come within the next four years. They encouraged me to get tested to be on the kidney transplant list. Through the grace of God, I was contacted to let me know that a kidney was waiting for me.

Tears rolled down my face and all I could say

was "Thank You Jesus!" It was my desire to receive another transplant so I could be on earth with my six-year-old granddaughter, see my grown children reach their goals as young adults, and support them in their adult lives as I did while they were younger. I was SO GRATEFUL! My children, family, and friends inspired me daily to keep on living!

My kidney transplant operation, the second of my two transplants, was on September 12, 2013. (According to the medical community it is not uncommon for transplant recipients to receive a second transplant).

Vicki, Pearl and Joy

CHAPTER 1

SHOCK!
WHERE IT ALL STARTED

We laugh, we cry, we make time fly.
The bond between us will never fall apart.
As is the mother, so is her daughter.
– EZEKIEL 16:4

Pearl Lambert speaks:

It all started on the fateful day of March 18, 2001. I walked into Dr. Vinod Rustgi's office with my daughter, Vicki. I was going to hear the final verdict about the liver complications which I had for the past two years. Vicki and I were called in to see Dr. Rustgi, who came into the office and looked at both of us. He had my medical chart in his hands and looked up at me. My heart started racing and I started shaking.

He said "Ms. Lambert you have a rare disease called Primary Sclerosing Cholangitis (PSC).

"It is found mostly among men, but women do have this disease." He also said the disease is often hidden for many years and it is detected when people are in their 40s or 50s. He began to explain what could slow down my disease.

He told me I would have to have a procedure called Endoscopic Retrograde Cholangio Pancreatography (ERCP) which would help slow it down, but the best option would be to have a liver transplant.

I looked at him and then at Vicki and said WHAT?

He repeated. My heart just dropped to the floor, and it was racing!

My eyes began to water with tears. I was thinking and asking myself, "What if I don't live to receive a liver transplant?" I was shocked! I was just in shock that I, Pearl, an ordinary woman trying to make it in this tough world, needed a liver transplant. As it turned out, working two jobs had taken a toll on my health.

I did not want to retire. I was very upset that I had to, especially because when I went to work at times I would feel better for a while. But then I started to go downhill even more. I lost my appetite and lost over 120 pounds! I have never lost that much weight in my life. I was wearing a size 16 and dropped down to a size 4. My skin and hands were getting very dark. My skin was itchy, which is a side effect when the liver fails. I was vomiting at least three times a day. I felt tired and weak. I had bleeding from my nose at night. I suffered from convulsions. I could not move around quickly. I was so tired, if I walked five feet I had to lie down. When I walked up steps, I would be tired; I had to stop at each step just to catch my breath and balance. I was dehydrated almost every single day.

Many days I cried, wondering why I was stricken with this disease with no warning signs and no reason. I just could not understand what was going on. I'm a person who is upbeat and outgoing, but this was tough to handle. I had a hard time accepting that I had liver failure.

Despite all my medical problems, I had an angel by my side who kept telling me we would be all right and we would find a donor. This angel was my daughter Vicki.

Vicki attended all my doctor's appointments. I'm a strong person, but with her encouragement, she kept me stronger.

Vicki took the time to research and learn as much as she could about my disease. She didn't stop for even a minute!

She motivated me to read and educate myself about my disease, organ donations, and transplants.

As I began reading about PSC, I felt better inside. Vicki and I continued to learn more about it. We discovered that Walter Payton, a famous football player, had the same disease.

Despite all the research and education, the disease continued to take a toll on me. I became weaker and weaker by the minute! At least every three days, I got worse. Vicki and my family were constantly running me to the emergency room. My symptoms were vomiting up fluids every five minutes, weakness, and dehydration. As soon as I arrived to the ER, the nurses and the ER staff would admit me right away because my blood pressure was extremely high and I needed fluids immediately.

I had to drink liquid meal replacements because I didn't have any appetite, and the doctors were worried about my nutrition. The doctors encouraged me to drink meal supplement shakes to help replenish nutrients in my body. Those shakes were just nasty! Vicki and my family worked so hard to help me get my fluids and food as much as possible.

Words are not enough to express the unconditional love that exist between a mother and a daughter.
— PANKAJ KUMAR

Pearl and granddaughter Joy

CHAPTER 2

FEAR AGAIN?

Fear not, for I am with you;
Be not dismayed, for I am your God.
I will strengthen you, Yes, I will help you,
I will uphold you with My righteous right
hand.'

Isaiah 41:10 New King James Version (NKJV) **10**

One day I was sitting at home on the edge of my bed and just wondering how long I would live. So many thoughts ran through my head. Can you imagine having an illness that makes you leave this world and you would not be able to see your family and loved ones? I thought, what if my heart just stops one day? What if my liver fails? How would Vicki and Ronnie handle me not being in this world anymore?

I was so frustrated with my condition and asked God, *why me?* Why was I chosen to have a life-threatening disease? I have always helped others and raised my two children. I just sat on the edge of my bed and cried and cried. You know, the spirit of Lord had tested me on this day!

I asked myself, *am I ready to leave this world?* More tears just rolled down my face. I was not ready to leave this world. I got on my hands and knees and I began to pray. I asked God to give me strength and mercy to get through the next part of my life.

After I prayed, my phone rang; it was Vicki. She began asking how was I feeling. She seemed to always call me when I was down. Sometimes I think it was the spirit of the Lord working in mysterious ways. Every time I had an episode that sent me to the ER she would happen to call. She would say, "Mom you need to go to the ER, you don't sound right." Of course, I would refuse. She would do a lot of negotiating with me. Sometimes she would just say "Mom, go to the ER and get better for Ronnie and me." She would hang up the phone, call me back and ask me if I was going to the ER. I would tell her. "Vicki, I'm going to be all right." Next thing I know, an hour later Vicki is knocking at my door. "Mom we are going to the ER and I don't care what you say. The doctors can help you feel better." So she would pack my things and we would go. Sometimes she would have her cousins (my nieces) with her. As time went on, Vicki would boost my self-esteem by saying, "Mom we must educate ourselves about your disease so we can ease our fears."

Vicki and I met several days later. She came to me with a piece of paper with a list of items to complete and a deadline date! She had goals that she planned for us. She said, "Momma, I want you to get to the library and get everything you can find, including stories about others in the same situations as you." Back then the Internet was not so popular, and many older folks didn't like the computer. So, I had to do my research the old-fashioned way. There was no Facebook or Twitter.

She planned for me to get out and get all the pamphlets and brochures and any information I could find from attending doctor visits. She also said, "When we go to our appointments, I want you to take the initiative to get all the information to help ease your fears." She even gave me a deadline date to find the information. I looked at her and said to myself, "She is absolute crazy! She must think I'm one of her students." My daughter was a high school special education teacher at that time.

At the same time, Vicki went on the Internet to research and understand the definition of this disease and find information relating to organ transplants. She decided that when we finished our homework we would meet again and put everything into perspective. She had many more goals and information typed on that piece of paper. She gave me colored paper to help keep me organized.

I was depressed, but my daughter just had a proactive mind, and was highly motivated to learn everything she could. Vicki is known to be highly focused when she wants to learn something or if she does not understand something. She will not stop until she gets all her answers. She will not accept "No" until she understands things and she loves to apply what she has learned.

The fear continued to race through my heart because I was still facing that I could leave this world soon. I was telling myself that if God calls me home, I would miss my family. As the first year went by, I began to get sick and needed medical care. There were many days that I did not want to go to the Emergency Room.

There were many nights that Vicki argued with me and begged me to go to the ER. She would call family members such as my nieces and nephews to help her convince me to go. I used to reject going to the ER because I feared I was not going to come back home. I used to think that the ER medical staff could not do anything to help me and I wasn't going to be on earth much longer, but I had faith and prayed. These thoughts were flowing through my head, but I did not express them to Vicki, knowing she was working so hard to keep me stable and comfortable. There were many nights that I stayed up all night because I thought if I fell asleep I might not wake up. I would watch TV all night. I would call and chat with Vicki about old times and review our appointments for the week. I would get so confused and could not remember the dates and times of the appointments. I would ask Vicki 100 times when my appointments were. Vicki would get frustrated, asking, "Mom, how many times are you going to ask me the same thing?"

Vicki Lambert speaks:

Why did I decide to help save my mother's life? Two months prior to my mother's first visit with her liver specialist Vinod Rustgi, we had been going back and forth to her primary care physicians and running all over Northern Virginia visiting specialists. Sometimes my mother's appointments would be thirty miles apart. I was getting tired every day. I maintained my full-time career as a special education teacher and worked part-time to earn extra cash to help with her medications that changed every time she went to the ER. I had to earn extra money to help with paying for gas to get back and forth to medical appointments. I lost leave time at work. Every single year I would be in the negative for leave. I would have to buy time from my employer's leave bank. There were days I had to take leave without pay.

Dr. Sullivan was my mother's primary care doctor and was very concerned about her. She was getting ill; her white and red blood cell levels were very low. Dr. Sullivan referred my mother to several doctors to rule out any other conditions. He thought she might have had some signs of cancer due to her low blood cell levels.

Mom always had such a busy schedule, she did not keep up with her doctor appointments; they became overwhelming for her. She was not responding because she was nervous about what the doctors would say. I wanted and needed to get more involved with my mother's health care to help her. Dr. Sullivan had to hunt my mother down for follow-up visits.

He had to search my mother's family members' phone numbers in her medical chart. He finally touched base with one of my favorite cousins, Sonya. She was also one of my mom's neighbors at that time.

After her phone call with Dr. Sullivan, Sonya told him that she would be sure to get Pearl the message and get her to contact him. Immediately, Sonya contacted me and told me that my mom was not returning her doctor's calls and they were trying to get in touch with her. Sonya thought it was time for me to step in and assist her with her medical appointments. Our family is known to look out for each other when we have crises. We all pulled together to take turns taking her to her medical appointments.

Dr. Sullivan had mentioned her blood levels were low. He was also concerned with liver enzymes, which were not showing the appropriate reading. He told my mother, "I am going to send you to one of my colleagues who specializes in understanding liver enzyme levels."

The last doctor he referred her to was Dr. Rustgi, a distinguished liver and hematology specialist in the Washington DC area.

The mother-daughter relationship

is the most complex.

WYNONA JUDD

Vicki and Joy

CHAPTER 3

VICKI'S SACRIFICIAL LOVE

"A Strong Love That Keeps Loving"
AUTHOR UNKNOWN

Thanks [be] unto God for his unspeakable gift.
2ND CORINTHIANS 9:15

Pearl Lambert continues:

Vicki and I were always close, from the time she was born. She was always concerned about her brother and mother. She loved us so much she would always say, "Mom, I'm going to better myself so I can help you and Ronnie out." She would help me a lot when her brother was young. Many days I struggled with my two children; I did everything possible to help them. My son used to have seizures all the time. We had to rush him to the ER two or three times a month from birth to about the age of 14! I had to go back and forth to the doctors so they could help my son with his cerebral palsy. Many folks don't understand cerebral palsy. My son had fluid on his brain when he was born. The medical community calls it hydrocephalus. I would always have Vicki with me because I didn't have a babysitter and I didn't want to burden my family with my children so I would do what I had to do. Vicki rode in the ambulance on many occasions. I knew that was stressful for a young child to go through. Sometimes Vicki would ask me if her brother was going to be okay. Her eyes would get watery because I knew she was worried about her brother. It was very stressful and hard raising a child with physical disabilities. I took care of my son until he was 21 years old. I chose to live in a county in Virginia that could provide the utmost services for him. Many social workers found it very hard to help my son become independent because he was with me for 21 years. Today Ronnie is very independent and lives in his own apartment that has accommodations for people with disabilities and in wheelchairs. I'm just so proud of my two children. They have both been through so much more than the average human being from birth to the present.

One day, Vicki took me to a doctor's appointment. When we were riding down the highway, Vicki said to me, "Momma, I should get tested to see if I am a match to donate half of my liver to you. Mom, you know I'm very resourceful. I have been reading about it and feel comfortable with the process. I just want to see if I qualify to help you feel better."

I told Vicki she could choose to be my donor. I was not forcing her to make that decision. In fact, I felt a little guilty about it. I didn't want her to go through all of that. I told her I would continue to stay on the waiting list, but Vicki made up her mind to be tested. She immediately went through the steps. Once she made up her mind, there was no stopping her. She was on a mission. Vicki was creative; she pulled family members together and friends. They all took turns in helping us and being right by our side. As I'm writing, tears are just flowing down my face. All I can do is thank God and love my family.

So Vicki kept pushing on; first she had to find out if she had the same blood type. Once we discovered that she was the same type, she had to have further testing done.

Vicki assured me that she was going to continue to get tested since her blood type was a match.

One rainy day, Vicki had to come to assist me with some paperwork and help me run errands. As Vicki got in the car she told me, "Momma, I'm a match!" I cried and cried and shouted "THANK YOU JESUS!" We both hugged each other tightly.

Vicki began to explain to me that she completed all the tests and discussed with my surgeons that she was a perfect match. Vicki kept assuring me that she would stick to her decision, but the doctors and the medical team also stated Vicki could change her mind up to the minute before the operation. But that wasn't going to happen. Vicki said to me, "Mom, all we have to do is set a date." It was getting close to Christmas time. I suggested to Vicki that we do the surgery after Christmas, but she said no because I was getting so sick.

At this point, Vicki and I were overwhelmed with doctor appointments. As time went on, we began to get the family involved more and more. Vicki coordinated family meetings a week before the surgery to explain the procedures. I was so proud of her; she had colored notebooks and folders, information sheets, and assignments for family members to sign up for.

She even got family and friends to attend some of the pre-op surgical appointments. During that time frame of preparing for the operations, I had a family of five living brothers and a sister. I had a total of 11 brothers and sisters and I was the youngest. At our family meetings, Vicki encouraged all our family members and friends to be involved so the operation could be a smooth success. Our surgical team said she had to reach out to them as soon as possible and see who could help us. They stated it could be very stressful. The hospital social worker gave us many tips on how to get the family involved.

Finally, the day arrived. Performed by Dr. Amy

Lu and Dr. Lynt Johnson, the operations took place simultaneously on different floors of the hospital. The doctors cut away just over half of Vicki's liver and removed mine. They then placed the new half into me and attached blood vessels to it. The operation lasted 13 hours. We had a local television show interview us, FOX 5 news in the Washington DC area. They did a cover story of our operation called the Gift of Life! We also produced a documentary of our story but we lost video tapes and contact with our producer. We hope to find him soon.

That year, I got the best Christmas present I've ever had, "THE GIFT OF LIFE." I'm so thankful for what Vicki did and I thank God! Since I'm retired now I use all my spare time as much as possible to help Vicki out with her daughter and my brother, who is aging. She and the Lord gave me second chance!

We left the hospital together on December 27. Both of our livers grew back to normal size within six weeks. We had decided from the start: we walked in together and we'd walk out together.

Vicki returned to work a month later; she takes

no medication and feels fine. "I just have a scar, it doesn't bother me," she said.

Vicki speaks:

Once we found out I was a match, there were many things I had to do. The doctors checked my heart and lungs. They also checked my mental health, to be sure I was ready to do this. I had so many questions for the doctors. One that I was very concerned about was whether I would be able to have children. The doctors assured me that having children wouldn't be a problem. They were right, because my daughter Joy was born in 2008. I named her Joy because we had so many critical issues going on in our family. I wanted a name to represent happiness.

After the surgery, my recovery wasn't too bad. The doctors told me to walk and do crunches to help with my healing process. I do remember that I went out too soon after surgery, when the doctors told me to rest. That wasn't a good idea because I was in chronic pain.

The thing that I remember most was coordinating

everything, getting mom to all her appointments, taking off from work, getting prepared. Thank God we had lots of family and friends willing to help. I organized family meetings to make sure everything would be taken care of.

Call your Mother. Tell her you love her.
Remember, you're the only person who knows
what her heart sounds like from the inside

RACHEL WOLCHIN

Pearl and Joy

CHAPTER 4

A SECOND SUCCESSFUL TRANSPLANT

Be completely humble and gentle; be patient, bearing with one another in love.
EPHESIANS 4:2

Vicki Lambert speaks:

In 2012, Mom began to have kidney failure. However, she was having kidney failure way back in 2008 before my daughter was born. She was placed on the national kidney transplant list.

Back in 2002 when my mother had her liver transplant, her medical team made us aware that she would have kidney failure 10-15 years after the liver transplant.

When her kidneys failed, I was taking her to the

ER from Alexandria, VA to Georgetown University Hospital. It was almost a repeat of what happened over ten years earlier when she began to have liver failure. She would get dehydrated and needed fluids to keep her stable. We were going back and forth to the doctors almost constantly. I saw her losing weight. At first, we didn't know what kind of problems she was having. I was hustling to get everything for her to be on dialysis and maintain all the tests she needed to stay listed on the national transplant list. I immediately made appointments.

My mom kept saying she was tired. I asked her if she was sure she wanted to go through with another transplant. I said to her, "Mom, it is going to be a great deal of work. We have to get organized like we did ten years ago and yes, we will be going to many medical appointments." I had to stress to my mother that it was imperative we make sure all tests were up to date so she would not drop off the list. I felt like I was racing to keep her alive. I knew we did not have much time because there was no function in her kidneys. Mom agreed and said, "Yes, I want to stay here longer to be with my family and friends." I told her we had to get going fast! It was so hard. It was hard to hold my tears back. She kept saying, "But I was doing so well and all of sudden I got sick." I could see the worry in her face. I could feel what she felt years ago saying to me "Is it time for me to leave this world?" My heart just ached to see her slow down again because she worked so hard to care for herself.

It was so frustrating. I didn't burden the family too much because I had flexibility in my schedule. It was a very emotional time for me. I just knew my mom was not feeling well and the only thing I could do was be proactive and help her much as I could. We would be up all night and Mom would vomit consistently. All I could do was comfort her as much as I could. I would ask her, "Do you want to go the ER?" She would say, "No, I'm going to be all right." I would have to call my cousin Sonya to ask her to help me convince my mom that she needed to get to the ER. She would lie down and 30 minutes later, she would be vomiting again. I took her blood pressure and it was not normal. We had to rush her to the ER. This would happen at least every three days. Sometimes I would have to take her to the ER and stay with her until she got admitted to the hospital. Then I would come back home and take care of my daughter, my uncle, and my needs. Mom would call me via video phone. She never used her video phone to make calls. At that point I knew she was feeling ill and seeing my face may have made her feel better. Sometimes I would think she was thinking in her mind she may not see me again. After our phone conversations, I would just get in my car and ride and cry. I just felt so bad for her. As I'm writing these thoughts, my eyes are tearing up.

I kept thinking to myself, "I don't think she is going to be here much longer." After that thought, I worked even harder for her because I know she did the same for her two children! Tears were rolling. I got organized. I pulled my resources and support team together. I stayed in touch with family to give them updates of what was going on. One of my mother's best friends, Charles helped us. I told my uncle I needed him to help get my daughter off to school. I told Mom we had to work hard and fast. I told her she had to be ready for numerous appointments and dialysis three days a week. I kept telling my mother she was going to have a kidney transplant. I knew she followed her doctor's orders and worked hard with the daily process when she was on the list in 2008. Back then, her kidney specialist said that her kidneys would fail within four years, and she needed to get on the list as soon as possible.

When Mom shares her story, people ask her why she had kidney failure. Many anti-rejection medications can wear on the kidneys. Kidney failure is one of the reasons many transplant patients have more than one transplant.

On September 12, 2013, while my mother was taking her daily walk, her mobile phone rang. It was the kidney coordinator at Georgetown University Hospital. The kidney coordinator said to my mom: "Ms. Lambert, we have a kidney for you."

My mom would never forget that day. The nurse told her she needed to get to Georgetown University Hospital right away. So, Mom called me. I was yelling and screaming! I was saying Thank GOD! THANK GOD! THANK GOD! Tears just rolled. I kept saying to my mother that I knew it was going to come because we worked so hard to maintain all of the medical appointments and followed all doctor orders. I knew my mom was good to herself because she worked hard at eating correctly and taking all her medications as prescribed on time daily. To this day she does that!

When patients have kidney failure, they need to have dialysis to help get the toxins out of the body. Planning and attending her dialysis treatment was very hard because I had to attend to my daughter's needs and take care of myself. Sometimes Mom would come home from dialysis feeling tired and weak. She had to stay with me for a short time to get her strength back. But we got through it by the grace of God. She was on dialysis for nine months before her kidney transplant.

While I was taking her to the appointments, I had to be strong and confident in front of my mom, my daughter, and my family. I did not want her to witness my emotions and wariness. I would cry, but I would just pray to God to give us strength. Sometimes, I would get in the car and take long rides and just cry.

I would take walks and cry and pray for strength for my mother and me.

I kept telling my mom in a very confident way, "Momma, you're going to get a kidney and you have nothing to worry about!" I told Mom not to worry about my hustle of taking care of her because I was raising my daughter as a single mother and caring for my uncle. I told her we were going to be right here by her side.

My mom had a second transplant on September 12, 2013. She had a kidney transplant from a deceased donor.

After the transplant, I visited her in the recovery room. She gave me a tight hug and said "Vicki, I'm so blessed to see your face and I'm just thanking God so much." She was crying and I was holding my tears back so she wouldn't have to worry about me. My mom said she was just so thankful that she got a kidney. All she could say was that she is so grateful! God had made a way for her again. "God gave me another chance!" She is so passionate about telling our story. She says she just wants to help other people.

Mom often tells me: "If I didn't have you I wouldn't be here." She hugs me tight and just cries.

Before my mom had the liver transplant ten years ago, we discovered that former football player Walter Payton had the same disease as she did. My mom said Walter Payton was famous; however, she felt she was just an average person working every day to make ends meet. And then, suddenly, she was struck by a deadly liver disease back in 2001.

My mom fights for her life every single day despite her two organ transplants. She is very organized and takes her medication on time every single day. She makes sure she doesn't run out of medications and follows up with her doctors. She eats a healthy diet. She is a very strong woman! She inspires me daily.

If you ask my family members and Mom's friends, they will tell you that while my brother and I were little she would always have us by her side. She loved her two children so much; they were the light of her life. I was extremely close to my mom as a little girl. If my mom left me with a family member or babysitter I would scream and cry and be so scared; my brother was a trouper; he never cried. We are still very close. My mother inspires me so much and she reaches my soul every day! She raised my brother who has cerebral palsy with no hesitation. She struggled with maintaining his health and helping us grow up.

After the kidney transplant, I touched base with one of my favorite cousins, Della, who has a nursing background. I let her know that the operation was a success. Della said, "Vicki! I know my Aunt Pearl is just fine. How are you doing?"

I said I was fine. She said, "Vicki you're so calm and you're not upset or emotional. I'm proud of you. You're a very strong person, and I'm just proud that you're handling everything so well."

*Being a parent means loving your children
more than you've ever loved yourself.*

ANONYMOUS

Vicki, Joy and Cousin

CHAPTER 5

A FAMILY LIKE NO OTHER

Love is patient, love is kind. It does not envy, it does not boast, it is not proud. It does not dishonor others, it is not self-seeking, it is not easily angered, it keeps no record of wrongs. Love does not delight in evil but rejoices with the truth. It always protects, always trusts, always hopes, always perseveres. Love never fails. But where there are prophecies, they will cease; where there are tongues, they will be stilled; where there is knowledge, it will pass away.

Corinthians 13:4-8

Vicki speaks:

My mom loves her entire family; she came from a large family of 11 brothers and sisters. Our family can have differences of opinion on each other's character, but we will always be there for each other regardless of any situation or crisis.

Before my mother was sick, I witnessed my uncles and aunts dying, year after year. I had a deep determination that I was not going to see her leave us at a young age.

One of my mom's older sisters passed away in her 50s. Her sister who was only two years older than her, Aunt Nannie, passed away. Aunt Nannie was there for us when we had our operation in 2002; she spent the night at the hospital to make sure that the doctors and nurses were treating us fairly. My mother said she would not leave our side and she would be right there for us. After Mom and I came out of the recovery room, we were on the same floor nursing unit for patients who just had transplants. We were right down the hall from each other. My Aunt Nannie would go back and forth to make sure we were stable and the nurses were treating us with excellent bedside manner.

Then she went home with us for three weeks to help us with recovery. She was like our personal nurse. We also had family members taking turns to help us. We always stress that if it weren't for our family and friends, we would never had gotten through this on our own. We had major support and love and we are so thankful! I could remember after the surgery all my cousin's best friends from college and other family was standing over me and embracing me with love and comfort.

My mother is proud of her two nephews. One is named Vincent, who prayed with her on speaker phone at the hospital. His prayers gave her a lot of strength. Vincent is a minister who lives in Alaska. Her other nephew, named Andre, is a local assistant minister of our family's traditional church, Walnut Grove Baptist Church, which my mother attends. When we touched base with him about the good news of the kidney transplant operation in 2012, he got in his car and prayed on the way to the hospital nonstop. He lives 45 minutes away from Georgetown University Hospital. All of our family members and friends planted the seeds in her soul to keep her living daily! She talks about them every single day. She spends as much time with her family as she can. At times, she gets sad because many family members have busy lifestyles and they don't have the time to visit with her and my uncle more often, because of the distance and the busy Northern Virginia culture. She drives one hour to church with her brother every single Sunday to visit her family and friends in Warrenton, VA. She hopes and prays that family and friends can visit and mingle more often not just on special occasions and during crises. I think going to church gives her courage to do what she must do every single day. She says she misses the old times at their church and how her mother kept the foundation of the family together when she was living. My mom has a brother named Uncle Nelson who lives in North Carolina. He encourages me and says I am doing a great job! My uncle in North Carolina is 79 years old. He would say, "Vicki, Pearl is a special sister and she went through a lot as an infant. She had chronic pneumonia a few days after she was born. The doctors told our mom that Pearl was not going to last through the night. So my mom's sisters hustled and walked to get medicine to help her survive."

Uncle Nelson thinks that Mom's medical conditions as an infant affected her later in life.

My Uncle Franklin, who is my mom's brother, close to her age, passed away several years ago.

Uncle Franklin was there after the liver operation. He came to the recovery room and kissed me on my forehead and said, "Vicki, thank you for helping to save my baby sister's life. I'm so grateful for you and God is going to bless you so much. You're a brave young lady."

He would always tell me this at family functions. I would run to the bathroom and cry but it would be tears of JOY!! I knew God gave me the courage to help my mom be in this world as long as she could. The family just thanks me so much and encourages me so much. When her sister, brothers, nieces, and nephews share their gratitude I feel so rewarded! I did not want the family to see me being emotional so I would always retreat at family functions, go in the bathroom and just say THANK YOU JESUS!! THANK GOD FOR MY FAMILY.

My mom's brother Durmia is an influence to all of us. He is 77 years old. He never had children but was always was there for his nieces, nephews, brothers, and sisters. I'm his primary caregiver along with family and friends that assist us. He would visit and take care of us on every holiday. Sometimes Uncle Durmia and I would go riding to take care of this and that. He would say, "I'm so proud of Pearl. She works hard to take care of herself. She takes her medications daily and she exercises and she follow her doctor's orders. Vicki, you are a special person. I'm so thankful for what you did for my sister and I'll do my best to help you all in any way I can." I would look over at him as we were driving and I could see tears rolling down his face. My eyes would water up. I would change the subject and turn up the music so we would feel less emotional.

My mom participated in a medical study after her kidney transplant to help newly transplanted patients who need anti-rejection medications after surgery, because she knew that it would help others. This was another way for her to show her gratefulness. I believe she is not ready to leave this world, and God keeps her here for a driven purpose which is to help others.

Joy, Pearl and Vicki

CHAPTER 6

OUR VOLUNTEER ACTIVITIES

Then the people rejoiced because they had offered so willingly, for they made their offering to the Lord with a whole heart, and King David also rejoiced greatly.
CHRONICLES 29:9

We are always grateful to God every day. Selfishness is not in our blood; we participated and engaged in many volunteer activities throughout the years to the present. In April 2012, we walked with the Kidney Foundation to help people like my mom. My daughter and a few cousins also walked in honor of people.

Our second year of participating was 2014. I'm so busy with taking care of the family and launching my own health insurance business and a travel business, that I could not put a lot of time into fundraising. However, the foundation is getting close to its goals. The Kidney Foundation is a wonderful resource for survivors of kidney disease and patients who have had transplants.

We also volunteered for the Washington Transplant Community. The website is www.beadonor.org. We do public speaking at events, along with running a table of information for the public regarding organ donation. Our big event was at the NBC4 Health and Wellness Expo, which attracts over 40,000 people in the Washington DC metropolitan area.

That's what people do who love you. They put their arms around you and love you when you're not so lovable.

DEB CALETTI

Joy and Pearl

CHAPTER 7

NOW IT IS YOUR TURN: DONATE!

Give, and it will be given to you. Good measure, pressed down, shaken together, running over, will be put into your lap. For with the measure you use it will be measured back to you."
LUKE 6:38

Vicki has done her part by donating what matters to the existence of her mother.

This is love, unconditional, unselfish, divine, and rewarding.

Do you have a passion to help those waiting for someone to help them survive?

Can you give your best resources in helping others when you can?

Someone needs your donation. People need donations.

We must realize people die daily from one disease or another because no one is ready help them. Many patients are still waiting in hospitals, hoping one day someone will come to their rescue. Where are the people this time?

Organs that can be donated at the time of your death include your heart, two lungs, two kidneys, liver, pancreas, and the small intestine. Organs can be used for life-saving transplants, research into cures for life-threatening diseases, and therapies for current disease treatments.

A typical organ donor is someone who has died after suffering a traumatic injury to the brain—for example, a stroke, an aneurysm, or a car accident. For death to be declared, a strict set of medical criteria must be met.

Among the criteria is the complete absence of activity in either the brain or the brain stem (responsible for reflexes such as coughing, gagging, blinking, etc.). By law, only a doctor not connected to the transplantation process may declare brain death. Some patients who suffer unrecoverable neurological injuries, but are not brain dead, may be able to donate after cardiac death.

After death by neurological criteria is declared, the heart, as a muscle, can still circulate blood for a limited amount of time and keep the internal organs viable. It is during that short amount of time that organs may be recovered for transplantation, research, therapy, and education.

The Washington Regional Transplant Community (WRTC) recovery staffs are notified about every death. If the patient is a potential donor, they will determine if the patient is registered to be a donor, approach the patient's family or health care agent to discuss the options of organ and tissue donation, and carry out the wishes of the donor or the donor's family.

We must all give, we must help our fellow man, no matter how seemingly small or unimportant it is ... A voice is crying! GIVE! GIVE!! GIVE!!!

Be an organ, eye, and tissue donor. You have the power to donate the gift of life.

Visit: http://www.beadonor.org/

TO GOD BE THE GLORY!

Joy

CHAPTER 8

VARIOUS MEDIA REPORTS ABOUT OUR STORY

For by grace you have been saved through faith. And this is not your own doing; it is the gift of God
EPHESIANS 2:8

SECOND CHANCE

As Reported By - Staff Writer, October, 2003.

Pearl Lambert and her daughter Vicki always shared stories, calls and visits. Now, they share much more.

They share an organ.

Last December, the pair underwent a relatively new procedure called a live liver transplant.

When a new liver became the only option to save Pearl, 53, Vicki decided to donate half of hers.

"She said, 'Momma, you gave me life, I want to give you life'," Pearl recalls during an interview in her Warrenton living room.

Seven months after Vicki Lambert donated half her liver to her mom Pearl Lambert, both are doing well.

During a routine annual check-up in 2000, her doctor noticed Pearl's liver enzymes were higher than normal. He ran blood tests, but nothing showed up.

Pearl went to a liver specialist — Dr. Vinod Rustgi of Fairfax — who diagnosed her with a very rare liver disease. Called Primary Sclerosing Cholangitis, the disease causes blockages in the bile ducts.

PSC prevents the liver from purifying toxins in the body and can lead to liver failure, cancer and ultimately death.

Dr. Rustgi told her she needed a liver transplant.

But Pearl felt fine. She worked full-time as a custodian for Fairfax County schools and as a part-time aide for Head Start.

"I didn't know what to say. I was like, 'Can you say that again? I need a liver transplant?' I couldn't believe it," Pearl says.

Dr. Rustgi told her to get on a liver transplant waiting list immediately at Georgetown University Hospital. She did. Two years passed and Pearl continued working two jobs. But by summer 2002, the disease began to take a toll. XI Toxins in her body would sometimes make her confused. She lost weight, vomited often and felt weak. Every three months, she had to get stints put down her throat to her liver to open the bile ducts.

But Pearl rarely complained.

"She's such a strong person spiritually and doesn't complain," Vicki says. "She won't complain."

Vicki, a 32-year-old special education teacher, had just moved to Prince George's County, MD. She wondered how she would take care of her mother.

Vicki began researching liver transplants and

learned about live donors.

"I got the courage up. The more I read, the more I felt comfortable about the process," Vicki recalls. But, first, she had to be a match for her mother. She was. The longer Pearl waited for a transplant, the sicker she would become. Pearl remained stable, but she faced a better chance of survival if she received a new liver soon.

Doctors scheduled the transplant for Dec. 17, 2002.

"I was just . . . it was a big thing to do," Pearl says. "It was up to her. I just thank God she did what she did."

Mother and daughter arrived at Georgetown University Hospital at dawn the day of the surgeries.

The operations took place simultaneously on different floors and lasted 13 hours.

Amy Lu and Lynt Johnson performed the procedure. They cut away half of Vicki's liver and removed Pearl's. They then placed the new half into Pearl and attached blood vessels to it. Within six weeks, both livers grew back to normal size.

Live organ donors face less than a 1 percent chance of dying. Recipients have an 85 percent success rate.

The first live liver transplant took place in Brazil in 1989. The procedure became more commonplace in the late 1990s. To date, more than 400 have been performed worldwide.

As soon as Pearl and Vicki woke up, they wanted to see each other. They spent Christmas in the hospital, surrounded by family who brought all kinds of food.

Family members proved supportive from the beginning, helping in any way they could, the women say.

"I said, 'We walked in together and we'll walk out together'," Pearl says.

The two recovered in Pearl's Warrenton home. Pearl's sister came from Texas to care for them. Mother and daughter shared a king-sized bed with pillows down the middle. They would hold hands over the pillows.

One month after leaving the hospital, Vicki returned to work. "I have no symptoms, just scars," Vicki says. "Everything else is fine." She takes no medication.

Pearl, however, will continue taking anti-rejection medication for the rest of her life. Following the surgery, she took 40 pills a day. She remembers 20 bottles lined on the kitchen counter top,

Pearl may never return to work; she retired last summer.

"I look all right. I feel good. I'll never go back to what I used to be," she says.

But it doesn't matter, really. She's been given a second chance. Because of her daughter, Pearl continues to live.

Now, the family faces the task of raising funds for her liver transplant. Insurance covered much of the procedure, which can cost up to $280,000.

"I'm on a mission for her not to reject my liver," says Vicki, an energetic young woman.

Part of her mission includes making sure Pearl gets her anti-rejection pills. The medication can cost more than $2,000 a month. Vicki wants to host a walk-a-hon to raise money. She also holds weekly meetings in Hyattsville, Md., at the Gospel Live Food and Entertainment Restaurant to rally folks together in awareness and to raise funds.

"The story doesn't ever stop," Vicki says. "The story keeps going."

WALTER PAYTON VERSUS PEARL LAMBERT

Transplant saves one resident, while another waits

BY GEORGE ROWAND, Democrat Staff Writer February 26, 2003.

It may not seem so, but football great Walter Payton and Warrenton resident Pearl Lambert had a lot in common. No, Lambert did not have the athletic ability of the Hall of Fame running back, whose moves were so smooth that he was known as "Sweetness."

What they shared was a rare liver disease. Because he could not find a donor liver in time, the disease killed Payton. Lambert, on the other hand, was saved by a little family intervention. Lambert's daughter Vicki, formerly a teacher at Fauquier High School, donated half of her own liver to her mother. Two months later, both Lamberts are doing just fine and both are well on their way back to health. Pearl Lambert suffered from primary Sclerosing cholangitis, or PSC, a disease of the bile duct. "This is a very rare disease for a woman," she said.

"They did a bunch of tests. We went from doctor to doctor to doctor. It took the doctors a while to find out what it was, but then they said that without a new liver, I would die." Lambert said there are two ways for a patient to receive a liver: from a cadaver or from a living donor.

Unlike any other organ, a healthy liver will regenerate itself if half of it is transplanted into the patient. Vicki Lambert said they held several family conferences to discuss the situation and to inform everybody about the prospects.

"This was a really long struggle for the family," Vicki Lambert said. "Then the doctor said that she needed a new liver, and I tested out as a perfect match. So, I told my mother, 'It's like me giving your life as you gave me life." The decision was made and the operation was set for Dec. 18 at Georgetown University Hospital.

The dual operations had to take place simultaneously, and went on for 13 hours. "It wasn't that bad," Vicki Lambert said. "It was my first time in the hospital and I thought that I wasn't healthy enough to do the operation, but I was." They left the hospital together on Dec. 27.

Pearl Lambert takes several pills every day to ensure that her body does not reject the liver; her daughter isn't supposed to lift anything heavy until she is completely recovered. They were giggling like school girls when interviewed.

Their experience has set them on a mission to raise awareness about the importance of organ donation, especially among African-Americans. "There are more than 80,000 Americans waiting for transplants, and a high percentage of them are African-Americans and Latinos," Vicki Lambert stated. "A lot of African-Americans don't believe in signing their organ donor cards. They feel that they want to take all their organs with them when they die, but they can save a lot of other people if they sign." The Lamberts also are raising $60,000 to pay their medical expenses. Pearl Lambert had to quit her job of 25 years with the Fairfax County school system when she got sick.

The liver is the only human organ that will regenerate itself. A donor gives half of his or her liver, and within three weeks or so, the liver is back to normal size.

"I really don't want to ask someone with children to give me half their liver," the doctor said. The NICV guidelines for a possible donor state that the person should be between 18 and 55 years of age, in good condition.

A Daughter Donates Half Her Liver to Mother Out of Love

ON THE MISSION TO EDUCATE

Lamberts speak out about organ transplants

As reported on: Wednesday, February 9, 2005.

Pearl and Vicki Lambert have a story and they want to share it with everyone they meet. The story has a happy ending, but could just as well have turned out otherwise, were it not for the decision made by Vicki Lambert and the successful procedure performed at Georgetown Hospital.

Pearl Lambert recalls how it all came about. Working two jobs, one as a custodian for Fairfax County and another as a part-time aide for Head Start, she felt just fine. However, a routine checkup revealed that was not the case.

"I went for a checkup and the doctor told me my liver enzymes were too high," Pearl Lambert said.

After extensive testing, Pearl Lambert returned to the doctor for his diagnosis.

"He said, 'Pearl, you have a disease. You need a liver transplant,'" said Pearl Lambert. "1 didn't know what to say. I felt fine; I was working two jobs and had no idea."

The disease, primary Sclerosing cholangitis, is a very rare liver disease that usually only affects men. Pearl Lambert can never remember the name and calls it PSC. All she knew was that it was attacking the bile ducts in the liver and was going to make her very sick. Walter Payton, Hall of Fame running back, had the same disease; he died from it because he could not find a liver donor in time.

"I read his book — I could relate to him. Just like him, I didn't want anybody to know and I didn't want anybody to feel sorry for me," said Pearl Lambert.

The diagnosing doctor, Dr. Vinod Rustgi of Fairfax, suggested that she get on a waiting list for a liver at Georgetown Hospital immediately. To buy time, Pearl Lambert spent the next two years undergoing a procedure every three months where a stint was put down her throat to open her bile ducts. After each procedure, she felt fine. Yet, the doctor's prediction that she would start to feel tired, start to lose weight, and get sicker and sicker would prove to be true.

"Everything he said came true," said Pearl Lambert. "You can be fine one day and get sick the next. I went from a size 13 to a size 4. I was still working — I didn't want to give up and tried to fight it."

THROUGHOUT IT ALL, Vicki Lambert was right there with her mother, taking her to the doctors and watching her getting worse. When she realized that it was possible for her mother to receive a liver transplant from a live donor, Vicki Lambert agreed to be tested. It was a perfect match.

"A lot of blood types don't match, but we were a perfect match," said Vicki Lambert, who decided that she wanted to go through with the operation.

"I'm a very practical person — my mother struggled to raise me and my handicapped brother and I was with her in the last stages of her disease. She got weaker and thinner — it hurt my soul. I told her, 'Momma, you gave me life; I want to give you life.'"

The transplant took place on Dec. 18, 2002. Performed by Amy Lu and Lynt Johnson, the operations took place simultaneously on different floors. The doctors cut away half of Vicki Lambert's liver and removed Pearl Lambert's. They then placed the new half into Pearl Lambert and attached blood vessels to it. The operation lasted 13 hours.

They left the hospital together on Dec. 27th. Both livers grew back to normal size within six weeks. Pearl Lambert said, "We walked in together and we'll walk out together."

Vicki returned to work a month later; she takes no medication and feels fine. "I just have a scar, it doesn't bother me," she said.

Pearl Lambert, however, continues to take anti-rejection medication and will do so for the rest of her life.

"I feel good. I'm still on medication, but not as much. I'm excited about it, and I want to help other people," said Pearl Lambert. "I want to get the story out to everybody."

They both volunteer their time helping the Washington Regional Transplant Consortium and speaking to groups.

"This experience has brought my mother and my family closer together. There are over 86,000 Americans waiting for an organ. The list is so long because people don't sign their donor cards," said Vicki Lambert, who is a new resident of Fairfax County and a special education teacher for Edison High School.

While Pearl Lambert won't ever be able to return to her job with Fairfax County — she retired with full disability, she will continue to be an active advocate for organ transplants.

"What I want to be is a spokesperson," said Pearl Lambert. "The more we come to the public, the more people who will donate their organs. Most people don't know about it. I want to tell my story and help somebody."

Vicki Lambert said that she and her mother have done a lot of public speaking, educating the public about organ donations. They have spoken at various churches, including Good Shepherd Catholic Church in Mount Vernon.

Vicki

Epilogue

Some folks ask how are we doing today, how do we feel.

Pearl speaks:

I'm not how I used to be, but I thank God every single day for giving me chances. I'm going to do everything in my power to take care of myself and help others. I live a blessed life. I work hard in giving thanks to God every day. I attend church in my home town every Sunday. I bring my brother to church with me every Sunday. Also, my friends and I do missionary work some Sunday afternoons. We go visit other church members who are ill. I help my daughter, as she is raising a beautiful little girl, my only granddaughter. My daughter Vicki is an ambitious young lady; she always wanted to be self-employed and have her own business. I help her out by taking care of Joy in the evenings after school or some weekends to give Vicki a break.

I also volunteer from 10-15 hours per month

when the assignments don't interfere with my church activities. I educate all people throughout the Washington, DC, VA areas, which we call the DMV area. The most important thing that I do is take care of myself and follow my doctors' orders.

I walk 30 minutes six days a week. I eat three meals a day. I drink plenty of fluids throughout the day. I take my medications daily, which is imperative. I remember from day one my medical team stated it is so important that patients take ALL of their medications. They explained to me in the very beginning that many patients have received transplants and felt better and did not take their medication as ordered. They also stressed those patients that did not take their medications, eat right, and follow their medical team's orders ALL PASSED AWAY!

As I'm getting older, like many Americans do, I have more medical needs to attend to. I make sure I do all yearly follow-ups and regularly schedule appointments.

I just can't thank Vicki enough for what she does for me and my family. Vicki helps me coordinate medical appointments and my volunteer activities. She goes with me on my medical appointments. She makes sure that my medications and needs fit my budget. If they don't, she is so resourceful she will pull her resources together and pull funds from her own pocket to help me out. I know it is so hard on Vicki, but she is such a caring and compassionate person. I work so hard to support her in meeting her goals and working her part-time business. I spend a lot of time with Vicki because I do worry about her, but my little girl has grown to be a successful woman. She amazes and inspires me daily.

Vicki speaks:

I'm fine. I just have issues with things that normal people in my age group have, such as struggling to maintain a healthy weight. I have no issue with my liver, and no complication from the organ donation 15 years ago.

I work very hard to help my daughter. I'm caregiver for an uncle who is aging. There was period where I felt down in my life, like any normal person would, but I got over it and kept pushing on. I had to leave my career of 13 years as a Special Education Teacher due to a work-related injury. This limited my physical standing abilities for a while. I gave birth to a beautiful baby girl eight years ago. I gave birth at the very late age of 37 years old, and had some challenges at that time. I named my daughter Joy to represent happiness in our family. I wanted to name her Joy so when we say her name aloud, it puts a smile on our faces. Joy is amazing; she is very, very smart. She can be very shy at times. She's extremely close to me. She's very attached to me like I was to my mother.

I oversee my medical needs. I'm busy person. I thought I could have a career as an entrepreneur so I could have flexibility in my schedule to take care of my family's and my needs.

I volunteer with my mom and Joy 2-5 hours per month. I'm learning how to have "me time." I'm so excited because I have found some resources to start traveling when it is time to take a break from life and just be me.

I also help consumers in the DMV area to enroll

in Affordable Health Insurance which was formerly known as Obamacare. This experience was the most complex thing I have done in my life, but my clients love my help. However, healthcare coverage may change and laws may change, so I must diversify my entrepreneur options as time goes on.

I try to maintain my health so I can be strong for myself and my daughter. I exercise three or four times per week. I go swimming once a week with my mom and daughter. I try to relax and socialize more and not to be so serious with business and taking care of the family.

I want to grow more as person so I can reach out to more people and make a difference in other lives. I listen to a lot of self-motivation books, authors, and speakers. I have made new friends and always surround myself with positive people as much as I can.

About the Authors

Pearl Lambert is 66 years old. She is a survivor of two donated organ transplants. Her daughter, out of love, unselfishly donated half of her liver over 10 years ago.

Just over three years ago, she received a second transplant, which was a kidney. She is extremely grateful and she wants to tell her story.

She is so thankful for daughter's gift and extremely grateful to the donor family that donated her kidney to her. Her daughter is also the co-author of her story.

Vicki Lambert is a healthcare enrollment specialist, speaker, and author. She educates individuals, families, and self-employed business owners on affordable quality health insurance. She is self-employed and works with the federal and state governments in enrolling consumers in Affordable Health Care. (ACA). She added a travel business to her self-employment portfolio.

Vicki graduated from Virginia Commonwealth University (VCU), with a Bachelor of Science Degree in Education. Her educational background, plus her working with the special needs population and living with siblings with disabilities, makes her an authority in understanding and relating to all people. She is passionate in helping people and extremely patient. She continues to be humble and pulls from her inner spirit and soul to help everyone in her path and does not expect anything in return. She says it is rewarding and a blessing to help others. She feels this is the reason she was put on this earth!

www.ingramcontent.com/pod-product-compliance
Lightning Source LLC
Chambersburg PA
CBHW071725040426
42446CB00011B/2218